HELLO, FROM THE CHILDREN OF PLANET EARTH

Don X Nguyen

BROADWAY PLAY PUBLISHING INC
New York
www.broadwayplaypublishing.com
info@broadwayplaypublishing.com

The world premiere of HELLO, FROM THE
CHILDREN OF PLANET EARTH was produced by
The Playwrights Realm (Katherine Kovner, Artistic
Director; Roberta Pereira, Producing Director) in New
York, opening on 7 March 2018. The cast and creative
contributors were:

WILLIAM .... Jeffrey Omura
BETSY .... Kaaron Briscoe
FREDDY .... Jon Hoche
SHOSHANA .... Dana Berger
THE FARTHEST EXPLORER IN THE UNIVERSE
.... Olivia Oguma

Director .... Jade King Carroll
Stage Manager .... Kara Kaufman
Set design .... Kimie Nishikawa
Costumes .... Ari Fulton & Loren Shaw
Lights .... Nicole Pearce
Sound .... Elisheba Ittoop

CHARACTERS & SETTING

WILLIAM, M, 35, *an aerospace engineer*
BETSY, F, 35, WILLIAM's *best friend in high school*
SHOSHANA, F, 35, BETSY's *partner*
FREDDY, M, 35-40, WILLIAM's *friend and co-worker*
THE FARTHEST EXPLORER IN THE UNIVERSE, F, *a space explorer. Should be cast as young as possible.*

Time: Fifteen weeks leading up to August 25, 2012.

The play takes place in various locations in Maryland, Washington DC, and Interstellar Space

(Space)

(All is dark except for the twinkling of stars.)

(Three beeps.)

[[[BEGIN TRANSMISSION]]]

(Lights up on SHOSHANA *and* BETSY *in bed, staring out.)*

SHOSHANA: So…um…I'm sorry I screamed in your vagina.

BETSY: Yeah that was unexpected.

SHOSHANA: I feel terrible! I was trying to give you one night of…I mean we're both so stressed…and you're so good at it and…I was trying to hold back my…but it just kept building and it had nowhere to go but out my mouth.

BETSY: And in my vagina.

SHOSHANA: Yes, in your vagina. Because really, isn't that what this whole thing is about?

BETSY: My vagina? Also why are we saying vagina tonight? That's so clinical.

SHOSHANA: YES!

BETSY: Yes…sorry, what are you saying yes to?

SHOSHANA: YES this is about your vagina and YES it's clinical because what we've been dealing with is very clinical.

BETSY: Don't worry, I'm gonna make that call.

SHOSHANA: I'm not worried about you making the call. I'm worried about…what if it doesn't work out this time?

BETSY: It will.

SHOSHANA: How do you know?

Betsy presses her nose and forehead to Shoshana's. They look into each other's eyes.

BETSY: Because I believe in us. Okay?

SHOSHANA: Okay. *(Beat)* I love you.

BETSY: I love you too. Now please stop screaming in my vagina.

SHOSHANA: Okay.

(THE FARTHEST EXPLORER IN THE UNIVERSE *appears.)*

THE FARTHEST EXPLORER: Vaginas are a lot like space. *(Beat)* Oh, you don't know who I am, do you? Sorry. I'm the farthest explorer in the universe. Wait, I have to play this first:

(THE FARTHEST EXPLORER *touches a golden disk on her chest and a recorded greeting in a foreign language plays:)*

THE FARTHEST EXPLORER: That's Persian for "Hello to the residents of far skies." I have greetings in fifty five languages. Wanna hear all of them right now?

(A long beep)

THE FARTHEST EXPLORER: Oops sorry, gotta go. Heading to interstellar space. I'll finish my thought at the next transmission. Talk to you in one-point-three million miles!

(The men's room at Goddard Space Flight Center, Maryland)

(WILLIAM *and* FREDDY *are in their respective stalls next to each other. All we can see are their feet.)*

WILLIAM: And JPL is like "we think you'd make a great candidate on our next project. Any interest?" And I'm like "You mean...Mars?" Can you believe it? Everything's going so well! And that's what terrifies me. You know? Freddy? Are you even listening to me?

(Snoring)

WILLIAM: FREDDY ARE YOU FUCKING SLEEPING?!!

FREDDY: What? No. I'm here man. I'm here for ya.

WILLIAM: You were sleeping!

FREDDY: Alright, okay? I'm sorry. POOPING MAKES ME DROWSY!

WILLIAM: Did you even hear a single word—

FREDDY: Yes William! Things are going great and you think it's terrible.

WILLIAM: I'm freaking out man!

FREDDY: You should be elated.

WILLIAM: I should but I know something bad is gonna happen. To go this well...consistently...without something terrible happening? Not a chance. That's why I haven't slept well lately.

FREDDY: Oh, you can't sleep well? Oh, poor fucking baby. I haven't slept well since 1997.

WILLIAM: That's very specific.

(Toilets flush. FREDDY and WILLIAM exit their stalls—or perhaps the stalls magically turn into WILLIAM's office. Either way, WILLIAM is at his desk, typing away. FREDDY writes out an algorithm on a white board.)

WILLIAM: Maybe I'm freaking out because I can sense a major life change? I'm about due. It's been seven years of living and breathing Voyager. Wow, seven years. You shed your entire skin in that amount of time. You know that? You're like a whole new person every seven years.

FREDDY: I wish you were a whole new person every seven years.

WILLIAM: And major life changes never go smoothly. That's why last night I had this nightmare that freaked me out.

FREDDY: Big deal. I had a nightmare too. About my ex-wife. She had a fan for a head. Like one of those oscillating ones?

WILLIAM: I don't care about your nightmare! I was talking about mine.

FREDDY: I deeply apologize for wanting to share a part of my life with you.

(A text alert)

FREDDY: Hello?

WILLIAM: Hang on, I just got a text.

FREDDY: You mean from a real person this time? Our moms don't count.

WILLIAM: IT IS from my mom, shithead. My friend Betsy called her trying to find me.

FREDDY: Betsyyyyy oooh a girl! Now we're talking. Is she hot?

WILLIAM: I haven't seen her since high school.

FREDDY: William, FACEBOOK that shit! That's what it's for. You get on it to see if your ex is still hot or not.

WILLIAM: She's just a friend.

FREDDY: Fine, your friend Betsy. What does she want?

WILLIAM: To meet up. My mom says she lives in D.C. now.

Wow, I had no idea.

FREDDY: Dude, Betsy wants to BONE.

WILLIAM: No she doesn't.

FREDDY: YES SHE DOES! She calls you out of the blue, which means her life is shitty and she wants to bone someone from a time when her life wasn't so shitty. It's common sense.

WILLIAM: She doesn't. I'm sure of it.

FREDDY: What makes you so sure? Do you have empirical evidence?

WILLIAM: Yes. She's a…she's…

FREDDY: What?

WILLIAM: *(Whispering)* A lesbian.

FREDDY: Why the fuck are you whispering?

WILLIAM: I don't know.

FREDDY: Well this is tantalizing news. Do you have any hot lesbian stories you want to share about your friend Betsy?

WILLIAM: Um…well, one time in college she wrote me this letter saying she kissed this girl.

FREDDY: William, that's called freshman year.

WILLIAM: It was more than that.

FREDDY: Fine whatever. Even if she's a lesbian, I still think she wants to bone. They're very curious about our goods. Why do you think strap-ons exist?

WILLIAM: I've never thought about why strap-ons exist.

FREDDY: Well maybe you should.

WILLIAM: What?

FREDDY: There once was this guy who met this girl at a Dave Matthews concert. They went back to her place and BOOM the girl's girlfriend was there and he was like SWEET! Three-way! And you know what happened? Do you? Do you know what happened?

WILLIAM: How could I possibly know what happened?

FREDDY: The girls pegged him with a strap on.

WILLIAM: Bullshit.

FREDDY: Strap-ons are popular for a reason. It's about control and other Freudian…stuff.

WILLIAM: Why do you know so much about strap-ons?

FREDDY: Because knowledge is power William! Listen to me. It's true. Women, straight or gay, they get bored of their sex lives and sometimes they want to feel what we feel, you know?

WILLIAM: That's the most ridiculous thing you've ever said.

FREDDY: I highly doubt that. Trust me, William. It's more common than you could ever imagine.

WILLIAM: I'm officially uncomfortable now.

FREDDY: I'm not saying you have to believe me. I'm just saying be open to the possibility. Be ready to RECEIVE whatever may come your way. And if that happens to be a THREE way with TWO lesbians that may involve ONE strap-on, you should definitely be open to that. That's all I'm saying.

WILLIAM: That's all you're saying?

FREDDY: That's all I'm saying.

WILLIAM: Please leave now.

(THE FARTHEST EXPLORER *appears*.)

THE FARTHEST EXPLORER: Here's one in Gujarati… (*Playing*) Translation: "Greetings from a human being of the Earth. Please contact." Please do! That's part of my mission. To make first contact with aliens. And when I do, I'll play this golden record. It contains humankind's greatest hits. It's a seemingly noble gesture. But sometimes I wonder if it's not. Like, what if me playing this golden record for aliens is equivalent to humans forcing their home movies on unsuspecting dinner guests. These humans' deep and sometimes overzealous desire to connect to others is, well…super cute. I shouldn't doubt their intentions. After all, I am their ambassador. Gotta represent. Onward!

(A dessert shop in DC)

(BETSY and SHOSHANA are seated at a table. BETSY is skimming a menu.)

SHOSHANA: So I say mom, get off my nut. What I'm doing takes time. What I'm doing is ambitious. This career I'm trying to forge. And I just got out of college.

BETSY: You graduated like ten years ago.

SHOSHANA: Exactly. Thank you. She doesn't understand it takes time to build a culinary empire.

BETSY: You know, you really didn't have to come.

SHOSHANA: Nonsense. This affects me too, babe.

BETSY: I was hoping to ease him into things.

SHOSHANA: You haven't seen him since high school, right? This is a big deal! And like we said in our vows, we're here for each other through sickness and health and big ass deals.

BETSY: That's not exactly how our vows went…but, since you're here, wanna share this "Can't Say No" sundae with me?

SHOSHANA: *(Grimacing)* Nnnnnnn….nnnnn…you know, I just can't say no.

BETSY: Ah there's that humor of yours. Can't wait for William to experience that when he gets here.

SHOSHANA: Yeah, WHEN he gets here. Where is mister punctuality?

BETSY: He just texted. He's a block away.

SHOSHANA: Ugh! Why do people text when they're a block away?

BETSY: Shana.

SHOSHANA: I'm just saying by the time you finish texting—

BETSY: Try not to grill him when he gets here, okay?

SHOSHANA: *(Grilling)* What do you mean grill him? I don't grill people. When have I ever grilled people? WHEN HAVE I EVER GRILLED PEOPLE?!!

BETSY: Shana. BE NICE. Shana?

SHOSHANA: My name is Shoshana, which is Hebrew for I don't wanna.

BETSY: Shana!

SHOSHANA: I'm joking! Of course I'll be nice. I'm gonna be so fucking nice!

(WILLIAM enters.)

BETSY: *(Waving)* William!

(BETSY stands and hugs WILLIAM.)

WILLIAM: Betsy!

BETSY: It's so good to see you!

WILLIAM: Yeah, you too.

BETSY: It's been…well, forever!

WILLIAM: Yeah forever. Sorry for running late.

SHOSHANA: Hi, I'm Shoshana.

WILLIAM: Hi. Umm…

SHOSHANA: So great to meet you. Sit.

(They sit.)

BETSY: William, this is my partner Shoshana.

WILLIAM: Oh! Partner. So you're both...well, you know.

SHOSHANA: *(Savoring)* Oh we know.

WILLIAM: Yes of course you know.

BETSY: Great, now we all know!

WILLIAM: And knowing's half the battle!

(Awkward)

WILLIAM: Bets, you look great. Just as I remember.

BETSY: Thanks, you too.

WILLIAM: I track everything I eat and drink. It keeps me optimal.

SHOSHANA: A well-oiled machine this guy.

WILLIAM: I try. I started tracking everything since high school. After I broke my arm. Remember that Bets?

BETSY: I remember the broken arm and the obsessive tracking, yes.

(They share a laugh.)

BETSY: Ah, Lincoln High.

WILLIAM: Go Links!

BETSY: *(To SHOSHANA)* That was our mascot. We were links, like in a chain.

WILLIAM: Unbreakable.

BETSY: Unbreakable.

WILLIAM: Wow, do you feel that? Everything feels so...

BETSY: I know!

WILLIAM: Like we just saw each other / yesterday.

BETSY: Yesterday!

WILLIAM: Psyche!

BETSY: Psyche!

(WILLIAM *and* BETSY *do some elaborate handshake.*)

SHOSHANA: I love that you two have a secret handshake. *(To* BETSY*)* Why don't we have a secret handshake?

BETSY: I didn't realize you were into secret handshakes.

SHOSHANA: *(To* WILLIAM*)* You'd think being together for five years, she'd know me by now.

WILLIAM: Five years. Wow. So have you been in DC this entire time? And who are you working for? Sorry, I try to gather as much data as possible. I'm sure it's annoying.

(SHOSHANA *takes* WILLIAM's *hand.*)

SHOSHANA: No, I love it. We should all get to know each other...thoroughly. Right?

WILLIAM: Umm...right.

(SHOSHANA *releases* WILLIAM's *hand.*)

SHOSHANA: I'm a chef at a farm to table restaurant in Columbia Heights.

BETSY: That's our neighborhood.

WILLIAM: Oh wow. A chef. Very cool.

SHOSHANA: Do you like to cook?

WILLIAM: Nope.

SHOSHANA: Oh.

BETSY: William, guess what I do.

WILLIAM: Hmm. Well knowing you, you're changing the world. Probably a non-profit?

BETSY: Probably? Of course I am. Amnesty International.

SHOSHANA: She's an Advocacy Director.

WILLIAM: That totally sounds like something you would do. It must be so rewarding.

BETSY: It is. It makes up for all the hard days. But... *(Beat)* "It is better to light a candle than to curse the darkness." That's our motto.

SHOSHANA: She loves saying that motto. My restaurant's motto is "You can't buy happiness, but you can eat local...and that's the same thing as happiness." We're still working on it. *(Beat)* Look, you'll have plenty of time to get to know us better. Let's talk about you, mister. What do you do?

BETSY: *(To* SHOSHANA*)* I told you he's an aerospace engineer.

SHOSHANA: Yeah, but like what's that all about? What do you do specifically?

WILLIAM: Well, I work at Goddard Space Flight Center in Maryland.

SHOSHANA: Hmm.

WILLIAM: Which is a part of NASA—

SHOSHANA/BETSY: *(Impressed)* OOH!

BETSY: NASA, wow.

WILLIAM: Yeah, I should've led with that.

BETSY: That's so great you're in this field. I remember you wanted to be an astronaut.

WILLIAM: Well, what boy doesn't?

SHOSHANA: Or girl.

WILLIAM: Right. Yes, of course.

SHOSHANA: So what do you do at NASA exactly?

WILLIAM: I maintain the firmware for Voyager 1.

(Off BETSY *and* SHOSHANA*'s non-response)*

WILLIAM: You know Voyager 1, right?

BETSY: A satellite?

WILLIAM: Well, it's a space probe. It's meant to explore deep space.

(Off BETSY *and* SHOSHANA*'s blank stares)*

WILLIAM: And so I maintain the firmware for it. And I upgraded their tracking software recently—

SHOSHANA: Because you like to track stuff.

WILLIAM: Yes, exactly. I'm one of the few who can program Voyager because it's so old. We're talking about the original code that was written in 1977! Like, the year *Star Wars* came out!

SHOSHANA: "Luke, I am your father!"

WILLIAM: Right. Yeah. That's actually from *Empire Strikes Back. (Beat)* Anyway, Voyager's expected to hit interstellar space this August. So I made, in my opinion, some very robust improvements to the tracking software which checks in with Voyager to see if it's still alive. I call it "Heart Beat" because you know, the heart…beats.

SHOSHANA: Well speaking of heartbeat, do you work out?

BETSY: Shoshana.

SHOSHANA: What? Health is important, right? It's good to be healthy.

WILLIAM: It is good to be healthy. Yes. I uh…I have a gym membership. It's free at work.

SHOSHANA: How much can you SQUAT?

WILLIAM: Squat? Uh…I'm more of a treadmill guy.

SHOSHANA: Oh cardio is good! Stamina's important.

*(*WILLIAM*'s not sure what to make of this.)*

BETSY: I watch all my terrible TV shows on the treadmill.

SHOSHANA: And on a scale of one to ten, how liberal would you say you are?

WILLIAM: Liberal? I'm pretty liberal.

SHOSHANA: Like an eight?

WILLIAM: Yeah. Eight. Eight sounds right.

BETSY: What does that mean? Let's discuss.

SHOSHANA: So, would you say you're willing to try new things? Get out of the ol' comfort zone?

WILLIAM: Comfort zone. Yeah, I could get out of the ol' comfort zone.

BETSY: Oh! Like our senior year business class! When you sold mechanical pencils dressed up as a pencil. A pencil selling pencils! That was INSPIRED.

WILLIAM: Sold out our entire inventory!

SHOSHANA: So William, you're adventurous.

WILLIAM: I mean, I do work for NASA.

SHOSHANA: Yes you do. Well, I'm just gonna come out and say it.

(SHOSHANA *takes* WILLIAM *and* BETSY'*s hands.*)

BETSY: Hey we should probably order something, you think?

SHOSHANA: I know it's a little unconventional…what we're asking you to do. But this is something we really, really want to try with you.

WILLIAM: Yeah?

SHOSHANA: I have a good feeling about you. And us. Together. Do you?

WILLIAM: Yeah.

SHOSHANA: That's exactly what we wanted to hear. So, Bets and I...well...we're ready to do it if you are.

(WILLIAM *looks at* BETSY. *She smizes painfully. He looks at* SHOSHANA.)

WILLIAM: Do. It?

SHOSHANA: IT.

WILLIAM: Oh wow. Wow.

SHOSHANA: Wow is right.

WILLIAM: Wow, I know people dream about this—

SHOSHANA: We constantly dream about it.

WILLIAM: Oh?

BETSY: Did I mention we should order something?

SHOSHANA: The thing is William, we want to make sure you're up for it. Not just physically but emotionally as well. No regrets.

WILLIAM: No regrets is my middle name.

SHOSHANA: None of us should regret this. Because you know, once you do it, there's no...undoing it. Biology, you know?

WILLIAM: Oh I know biology.

SHOSHANA: Yeah, all the forces unleashed. Crashing into each other. Like that Dave Matthews song.

WILLIAM: Dave Matthews.

SHOSHANA: Right?

WILLIAM: Dave Matthews.

SHOSHANA: Yeah.

WILLIAM: I never used to be a big Dave Matthews fan...

SHOSHANA: Well I wouldn't say I'm a huge fan—

WILLIAM: But I guess I could learn to...embrace him, you know?

SHOSHANA: Umm…what?

WILLIAM: I mean doesn't everyone need a little…Dave Matthews in their life?

SHOSHANA: Umm…sure.

WILLIAM: *(Breathing)* Yeah. I think I could do this. I think I could receive some Dave Matthews.

SHOSHANA: *(To BETSY)* Why's he obsessed with Dave Matthews?

BETSY: He doesn't know.

SHOSHANA: Bets? *(To WILLIAM)* Do you know?

WILLIAM: I…think I know.

SHOSHANA: *(To BETSY)* He has to know.

BETSY: *(To WILLIAM)* You don't know.

WILLIAM: *(Confident)* Oh, I think I know.

BETSY: YOU DON'T KNOW.

WILLIAM: *(To BETSY)* I don't know?

BETSY: *(To SHOSHANA)* I didn't tell him.

SHOSHANA: What? Betsy! You said you were gonna take care of this!

BETSY: I WAS taking care of this, but then you showed up! You weren't supposed to be here, remember?

SHOSHANA: I couldn't keep away. You'd want to be here too, if you were me.

BETSY: Just…trust me to do this, alright?

SHOSHANA: Okay. *(To WILLIAM)* Wow, sorry William. You must have been so confused.

(WILLIAM *tries to play it off but is totally confused.)*

SHOSHANA: I mean, here's your friend who you haven't seen since high school and her partner talking about… well you know.

(WILLIAM *says nothing.*)

BETSY: *(To* SHOSHANA*)* This is what I was afraid of. Look at him, he's so confused.

SHOSHANA: Yeah, but he didn't seem confused. *(To* WILLIAM*)* Wait, you were going along with us. Right?

WILLIAM: Um...

SHOSHANA: If Betsy never told you, then what did you think we were asking you to do?

(FREDDY *appears eating Cheetos.*)

FREDDY: They want you to do what?

(WILLIAM*'s office*)

WILLIAM: You heard me.

FREDDY: And you thought they wanted...

WILLIAM: Yeah.

FREDDY: *(Laughing)* Oh man. William. Thank you. Thank you. I needed that. That's some funny shit, and I need some funny shit in my life right now.

WILLIAM: Yeah laugh it up. Just remember you're the one who put the stupid idea in my head!

FREDDY: I take full responsibility for spicing up your life. Lord knows you need it. *(Beat)* So they want you to be a donor daddy.

WILLIAM: Yep.

FREDDY: Make a withdrawal from the ol' spooge bank.

WILLIAM: Can I just remind you that we are at NASA?

FREDDY: I know, amazing, right? *(Beat)* So what be the terms?

WILLIAM: Terms? What do you mean, terms?

FREDDY: You gotta know the terms. No one hands out a loan without knowing the terms of the agreement.

WILLIAM: You make it sound like a transaction.

FREDDY: This IS a transaction, William. Of the sperm-mumental kind. *(Beat)* So which way is your penis leaning?

WILLIAM: I don't know. I mean, it's the most flattering and terrifying thing anyone has ever asked of me.

FREDDY: William, we make things go up into space. That's terrifying. This? This is what we were designed to do. Sprinkling the world with tiny versions of us.

WILLIAM: I just thought if I ever had a kid it would be with my wife.

FREDDY: You don't have a wife.

WILLIAM: I know I don't have a wife.

FREDDY: You don't even have a girlfriend.

WILLIAM: Thanks for the reminder of society's absurd notion that if you're single you're somehow "behind the eight ball of life."

FREDDY: Oh are we speaking in metaphors now? Is that today?

WILLIAM: Just shut up for a second. I'm thinking.

FREDDY: Should I take cover?

WILLIAM: You know, I thought I could have it all. But what does that really mean? A good career? A family? I focused on my career first because having a family was always something I'd do later in life. But later...is now. *(Dread)* And it has come for me. Maybe that's what my nightmare was trying to tell me. That my life is over just when it was getting good.

FREDDY: Well let's not dive into a black hole of despair just yet. That was a metaphor by the way. You're confused because you don't have enough data. You should talk to them about terms.

WILLIAM: Data. Right. I'm lacking data.

FREDDY: And excitement. I would be excited. Being a dad is something I've always wanted. The idea of legacy and—

WILLIAM: Hey! You know what? I'll write a program.

FREDDY: No.

WILLIAM: One that weighs all the pros and cons, just to make sure my decision is sound. I could use a Bayesian inference algorithm to power it. Wouldn't that be cool?

FREDDY: Or you could just use this. *(He pulls a magic eight ball out of* WILLIAM's *desk.)*

WILLIAM: I'm being serious.

FREDDY: Don't deny the power of the magic eight ball. It knows. *(Beat)* Fine. Write your little program if you want, but in the meantime, call the ladies up, tell them we wanna meet and discuss terms.

WILLIAM: We? Why do you have to be there?

FREDDY: I can help negotiate. You walk into the situation without proper knowledge, it won't end well.

WILLIAM: How bad could it be?

*(*THE FARTHEST EXPLORER *appears, dodging an asteroid.)*

THE FARTHEST EXPLORER: Whoa! That was close. I don't think I need to tell you how much Asteroids suck. Hurtling at twenty-eight thousand miles per hour hellbent on destroying anything that gets in their way. Beware of hellbent asteroids. They're everywhere. That's what killed the dinosaurs on Earth. That's what will probably kill civilization. If you stop to think about it, life on Earth is just…the space between catastrophes. Okay BYE!

(The Prospect)

(A cowboy-themed restaurant in Washington DC.)

(WILLIAM *is drinking a Lonestar.* FREDDY *drinks a margarita. There's a plate of calamari on the table.*)

WILLIAM: Of all the bars in DC, why'd you pick this one?

FREDDY: It's rugged. Aren't they rugged?

WILLIAM: Why do you think they're rugged? Nevermind, don't answer that.

FREDDY: So where are they?

WILLIAM: (*Checking his phone*) She texted. They're a block away.

FREDDY: Why the fuck would anyone text a block away?

WILLIAM: Stop.

FREDDY: I'm just saying, by the time they finish texting—

(BETSY *and* SHOSHANA *enter.*)

WILLIAM: Oh that's them. Freddy, this is Betsy and this is Shoshana.

FREDDY: M'ladies.

BETSY: Nice to meet you.

SHOSHANA: Hi.

(*Re: the cow on the wall*)

SHOSHANA: Nice…horns.

BETSY: So what's everyone drinking?

WILLIAM: Lone Star.

FREDDY: It's Texas piss. Get a rita. Ritas are what you want.

SHOSHANA: I guess two "ritas" for us.

WILLIAM: Gotcha. I'll grab them from the bar. Faster.

FREDDY: I'll take another one.

BETSY: *(To* WILLIAM*)* Oh, I'll go with you. Help you carry.

SHOSHANA: *(Pointing to* FREDDY*)* Why can't he go?

FREDDY: Freddy doesn't wanna go.

WILLIAM: It's alright. We won't be long.

*(*WILLIAM *and* BETSY *exit.)*

FREDDY: Sup?

SHOSHANA: Sup.

(Awkward silence. SHOSHANA *checks her phone.)*

*(*FREDDY *stuffs as much calamari as possible into his mouth.)*

FREDDY: Twenty calamari!!! *(Beat)* You know what's cool about an octopus? Their testicles are located in their head. They are literally dickheads.

SHOSHANA: Calamari is squid, not octopus.

FREDDY: No shit? Huh. *(Beat)* So, do you watch?

SHOSHANA: What?

FREDDY: The L Word. Do you watch it?

SHOSHANA: *(Feigning sexy)* Oh you mean the hot lesbian show?

FREDDY: YEAH!

SHOSHANA: NO! You think because I'm a lesbian, I watch the L Word?

FREDDY: *(Serious)* No, I just thought you might want to discuss some groundbreaking television. Jesus, I'm sorry.

SHOSHANA: So you watch it?

FREDDY: I own it.

SHOSHANA: You realize that show ended over three years ago?

FREDDY: *(Fondly)* Yeah. Instant classic.

SHOSHANA: I bet you masturbate a lot.

FREDDY: Like a baboon. Do you like baboons?

SHOSHANA: Not anymore.

FREDDY: Touché! I like your wit.

SHOSHANA: I like my wit too.

FREDDY: You know, we want the same thing here.

SHOSHANA: How could that possibly be true?

FREDDY: We want what's best for those we care about. So here we are.

(WILLIAM and BETSY enter with drinks.)

WILLIAM: Here we are!

SHOSHANA: I'VE NEVER WANTED A DRINK SO BADLY IN MY LIFE.

WILLIAM: Three margaritas. Okay, well, down the hatch.

(They all cheers.)

FREDDY: The ol' baby hatch!

(The cheers is ruined.)

WILLIAM: *(Ignoring FREDDY)* So, I don't really know how to do this.

FREDDY: I got this. First you'll talk about expectations, what each party wants and then you'll draft up a legal agreement. We want to make sure William is protected in case something happens. Like you decide to sue him for child support.

WILLIAM: I'm sure they wouldn't do that.

SHOSHANA: Of course not.

BETSY: We'll have something drafted up.

FREDDY: Great. I just want to make sure William is fully aware.

WILLIAM: And just to get this out in the open…if I decide to do this, I'm leaning towards not being involved.

SHOSHANA: That's perfect. That's what we assumed. *(To* BETSY*)* Right?

BETSY: Sure. But you're talking financially or legally, right? If you want to see the baby, you can be uncle William. We'd be happy with that.

SHOSHANA: Yep, we discussed it and that would totally be fine.

WILLIAM: Well that's good to know. But there's a good chance I might be working on the mission to Mars.

BETSY: That's exciting.

WILLIAM: Very exciting. It also means relocating to JPL in California.

FREDDY: That's Jet Propulsion Lab. Of NASA.

BETSY: So California?

WILLIAM: Yep.

SHOSHANA: Will you be taking someone with you? Or leaving someone behind?

FREDDY: Just me.

BETSY: I guess I never thought to ask if you had someone special in your life. That's so shitty of me.

FREDDY: He totally doesn't. He's as single as a slice of Velveeta. *(Beat)* You know, like those individually wrapped slices? Totally single, this guy.

WILLIAM: I prefer the term Independent Adventurer.

FREDDY: Yeah, well, he's very independent in his adventures.

BETSY: Are you sure California is where you want to be?

SHOSHANA: *(To* BETSY*)* Babe…

BETSY: I just want William to really think it through. Before he completely writes off his child.

SHOSHANA: Our child.

(Awkward)

FREDDY: Well this might be a good time to talk about timeline. As in…what's your timeline?

BETSY: We were hoping to start in about a month.

WILLIAM: A month? Wow.

FREDDY: That's a pretty aggressive schedule.

SHOSHANA: We've been thinking about this for a long time.

FREDDY: But why are you in such a hurry?

SHOSHANA: You mean besides being thirty-seven and a woman?

FREDDY: Hey I don't see age or gender. I just see people. Beautiful people of all walks of—

SHOSHANA: Am I imagining him? You can both see him, right?

BETSY: William, after our third attempt didn't work out, we're down to the wire here.

SHOSHANA: Bets!

BETSY: He should know.

WILLIAM: Oh, so…I thought I was your…but I guess I'm not.

BETSY: I'm sorry William. That's because we haven't seen each other in a long time.

WILLIAM: I see. So you said you've had three attempts. Does that mean…

BETSY: I've had three miscarriages.

SHOSHANA: Bets.

BETSY: It's okay. The last attempt was an IVF and since we can't afford another one…we wanted to try one more time at home. With someone I know. Someone familiar that I trust.

FREDDY: *(Pointing to* WILLIAM*)* This guy right here!

WILLIAM: Freddy.

BETSY: It's true. You're it, buddy. If you want to.

(Off WILLIAM's *silence)*

BETSY: Listen, the odds aren't great. But there are a lot of women who inseminated at home after a failed IVF—

SHOSHANA: And then went on to have children.

BETSY: Right. So we want to give it a shot.

WILLIAM: Sounds like there's a good chance this may not even work.

BETSY: There's a big chance.

WILLIAM: Listen I…this is new data that I think I need time to process.

(Beat)

BETSY: Sure. Take all the time you need.

SHOSHANA: Well, wait, we should probably set a deadline right?

BETSY: William can take all the time he needs.

WILLIAM: I'm gonna grab another drink. Does anyone want anything?

BETSY: No, we're good.

WILLIAM: Okay, I'll be right back. *(He exits.)*

BETSY: You know, I'm just going to go check on him.

(BETSY exits. FREDDY and SHOSHANA sit in silence. He offers her some calamari. She takes one.)

(THE FARTHEST EXPLORER appears.)

THE FARTHEST EXPLORER: *(Big happy sigh)* There's something to be said for going it alone. Many great explorers have done this with much success. Pytheas sailed the Arctic and associated ocean tides with the moon. Alone. Amelia Earhart flew across the Atlantic Ocean. Alone. Laura Dekker was the youngest person to circumnavigate the globe. Alone. Not lonely. Alone as in the freedom to do whatever I want, when I want. I'm so glad I'm by myself. This makes decisions less complicated. Not less hard. Just less complicated. Because you don't have to compromise with anyone. Sure, there are times I question this…but then I think of all the time couples waste trying to decide where to eat. *(Exits and comes back)* Which is an average of a hundred and thirty-two hours a year. You're welcome.

(BETSY and SHOSHANA's loft)

(BETSY is looking for her phone, running late. SHOSHANA helps.)

SHOSHANA: Three weeks.

BETSY: Can we stay on task please?

SHOSHANA: It's been three whole weeks.

BETSY: I need to find my phone.

SHOSHANA: And not a word from him.

BETSY: This conversation? Not helpful. Finding my phone? Very helpful.

SHOSHANA: You know what's not helpful? Mr. Spaceman's radio silence.

BETSY: Why are you giving up on William after only three weeks?

SHOSHANA: Um, I think he's given up on us. Or maybe you have.

BETSY: What the hell is that supposed to—

SHOSHANA: Have you reached out to him at all? I didn't think so.

BETSY: He'll come through. I know he will. This is what he does. He goes away and then he comes back. Don't worry. William and I will handle this.

SHOSHANA: I just want to remind you this is not about you and William. It's about us.

BETSY: Of course it is. I know this is hard for you. But I'm doing the best I can here.

SHOSHANA: It's bad enough that I can't carry the baby…

BETSY: It's not your fault. Hey. *(Beat)* It is the fault of biology. And because of biology, we can't do this without William. So right now, it has to be about him. But I guarantee you, I'm doing this for us.

SHOSHANA: You promise?

BETSY: *(Finding her phone)* Yes! I found my phone. But also yes I promise. Babe, I gotta go.

SHOSHANA: Fine. Go.

(BETSY stays.)

SHOSHANA: It's okay. I know you're late for work. Go.

(BETSY crosses to SHOSHANA.)

BETSY: No. This is more important. So what else?

(Beat)

SHOSHANA: I thought he'd say yes. Doesn't it worry you? That he's so hesitant?

BETSY: He takes a long time with big decisions. But trust me, once he decides, that's it. No backing out. Does that make you feel any better about him?

SHOSHANA: Not really. But it makes me feel better about you.

BETSY: Well that's a start.

SHOSHANA: For the record, I don't dislike William. I just don't know him the way you do.

BETSY: Maybe you should get to know him?

SHOSHANA: Oh what, like hang out with him? Maybe we can watch some Star Wars together?

BETSY: Great idea! I've never seen Star Wars.

SHOSHANA: Does William know that?

BETSY: No. And he never will. Okay?

SHOSHANA: Okay.

BETSY: Okay. I really gotta go now. Bye.

SHOSHANA: *(Joking)* Or I could just pop up at his work. Watch him in action doing whatever it is that he does at NASA.

BETSY: Probably not a great idea.

SHOSHANA: I was joking. I would never just show up at his job.

BETSY: You've done crazier things.

SHOSHANA: C'mon give me a little credit.

(WILLIAM'*s office)*

(SHOSHANA *and* WILLIAM *are seated with coffee.)*

WILLIAM: So this is…an unexpected surprise.

SHOSHANA: So how's your heartblip?

WILLIAM: My what?

SHOSHANA: That software program you wrote. For Voyager.

WILLIAM: Oh. My heartbeat. Wow, you remember that?

SHOSHANA: I saw an article on Voyager yesterday and it triggered my memory.

WILLIAM: Yeah, the media's finally paying attention to it. It'll be cool to read about it in history books someday. "In August 2012, Voyager 1 reached interstellar space, making it the farthest human made object from Earth."

SHOSHANA: That's great. You're gonna be famous.

WILLIAM: Well, Voyager will be famous. For a fleeting moment.

SHOSHANA: How does that make you feel?

WILLIAM: Grateful for fleeting moments I guess.

(Beat)

SHOSHANA: So Mars. That's exciting! Are you actually going to Mars?

WILLIAM: No, I'll just be working at Mission Control. Hopefully. If everything goes well with Voyager.

SHOSHANA: And what's the deal with Mars? Is it about colonizing it or finding Martians or what?

WILLIAM: Well I'm sure it's that way for some people. But for me personally, it's about exploring. We haven't done that in a long time.

SHOSHANA: Really? What about the Space Shuttle?

WILLIAM: That's not really exploring. That was delivering satellites and conducting experiments in space. Near Earth. Mankind physically has never gone further than the Moon. And that was in 1969.

SHOSHANA: Oh, wow, that long ago?

WILLIAM: Yep.

SHOSHANA: Listen, William, I don't mean to—

FREDDY: *(From the hallway, melodically)* Yo what time is it? It's poop time! What time is it? It's poop time! *(He enters.)*

FREDDY: Oh shit.

SHOSHANA: *(To* FREDDY*)* Hello.

FREDDY: Heyyy. I'm Freddy.

SHOSHANA: I know. We met like three weeks ago.

FREDDY: Right. Yeah. You're...Shanda.

SHOSHANA: Shoshana.

FREDDY: Right. Shanda is short for Shoshana. I have Hebrew friends. Impressed?

SHOSHANA: That you have friends? Yes.

FREDDY: *(Laughing)* See, that's great. I admire that. Humor in spite of persecution.

SHOSHANA: Oh my God.

WILLIAM: Freddy, can you give us a few minutes please?

FREDDY: Sure. *(To* SHOSHANA*)* I bid you adieu m'lady. *(To* WILLIAM*)* I'll be in the...men's room.

WILLIAM: No just go to your office.

FREDDY: But we always meet—

WILLIAM: Go to your office!

*(*FREDDY *exits.)*

SHOSHANA: Do you guys...go to the bathroom together?

WILLIAM: NO. Absolutely not. That's just code for...we have a meeting. A confidential meeting. Which is why he can't say outright that it's a meeting. Because it's confidential—

SHOSHANA: Yeah, okay I get it.

WILLIAM: Yeah, so I guess I should…

SHOSHANA: Yes, of course. I'll let you get ready for your secret poop meeting.

WILLIAM: It was good seeing you.

SHOSHANA: So, I'll tell Betsy you said hi?

WILLIAM: Yes. Absolutely. Tell her I said hi.

SHOSHANA: Is there anything else I should tell her?

WILLIAM: Umm…no, I don't think so. I'm still thinking things through.

(SHOSHANA *nods and then heads for the door.*)

SHOSHANA: Listen, you like *Star Wars*, right?

WILLIAM: I LOVE *Star Wars*.

SHOSHANA: Well, you are Obi-Wan Kenobi. You're her only hope.

WILLIAM: Are you saying Betsy is Princess Leia?

SHOSHANA: Duh.

WILLIAM: But Princess Leia wanted Obi-Wan to help destroy the Death Star, not get her pregnant. Star Wars is not about getting someone pregnant.

SHOSHANA: Star Wars ends with a tiny torpedo getting shot into a tiny hole in the Death Star and then it explodes and all of humanity is saved. Star Wars is about sperm donorship.

WILLIAM: *(Perplexed)* I need to get to…Freddy's waiting. *(He gathers his things.)*

SHOSHANA: William. If I could carry this baby myself, I would. But the doctors say I can't. So it's all on Bets.

And she wants this baby. And so do I. You're OUR
only hope.

(THE FARTHEST EXPLORER *appears.)*

THE FARTHEST EXPLORER: This is probably a good
time for me to finish my earlier thought about how
vaginas are a lot like space. Did you think I forgot?
You're right, I totally did. Been kinda busy. So, why
are vaginas a lot like space? Because life. Life originates
from both. You probably already know this about
vaginas. At least I hope you do. But space. Well, there's
the big bang and the creation of matter and stardust.
The odds of life being created out of all this chaos
are mathematically improbable, but it still happened.
Humans happened. All thanks to space. And vaginas.

(An alley)

(Late evening. BETSY *is taking out the trash.* WILLIAM *steps
out from the shadows.)*

WILLIAM: Hey there—

(BETSY *throws the trash bag at* WILLIAM.)

BETSY: NOT TODAY MOTHERFUCKER!

WILLIAM: Bets! It's me!

BETSY: William? What the hell are you doing out here?

WILLIAM: I was just…hanging around in the waning
gibbous of your building.

BETSY: What the hell is a gibbous? Is it still here?

WILLIAM: No! Sorry. Moon humor. Which I realize is
not appropriate at this moment. *(Beat)* I was gonna
buzz you but you came out here. Again, sorry.

BETSY: It's okay. So what brings you to a dark alley in
the middle of the night?

(WILLIAM *says nothing.)*

BETSY: William?

WILLIAM: Why me, Bets? After all these years?

BETSY: Are you sure you want to discuss this out here?

WILLIAM: I have to know. Please.

(Beat)

BETSY: Okay. Well, you are intelligent...passionate... loyal. Shall I go on?

WILLIAM: Please do.

BETSY: Persistent. Kind. And you accept me for who I am. I want my baby to have those same good qualities that you have.

WILLIAM: You see all of those qualities in me?

BETSY: I do.

(WILLIAM says nothing.)

BETSY: William?

WILLIAM: Remember your parents?

BETSY: Of course I do, they're my parents.

WILLIAM: Sorry, I just mean...your parents were always so nice to me.

BETSY: They were nice to everyone. But you especially.

WILLIAM: My parents couldn't be at my Boy Scout induction ceremony, so your parents stood in for mine. And that one summer your parents shuttled me back and forth to math camp for a whole week because my parents were too busy working.

BETSY: Out of all my friends, you were their favorite.

WILLIAM: Really?

BETSY: Don't play dumb. My parents loved you and you knew it.

WILLIAM: Yeah, I did. I do.

(Beat)

BETSY: What's going on?

WILLIAM: I don't think I'm capable of caring enough, Bets. Not the way your parents care. They're amazing at it.

BETSY: Why do you think you're not capable?

WILLIAM: If I go ahead with this and decide to be involved, I'm scared other parts of my life will pull me away and I'll just disappear from you and the baby. I'm scared that when the time comes, I won't be capable of caring enough. And that terrifies me.

BETSY: I'm telling you right here and now, you are capable of caring enough.

WILLIAM: If that's true, why did I let so much time go by without seeing you?

BETSY: Listen to me. It's not about the years. You didn't have to respond to my text. You didn't have to agree to meet me and Shoshana. You didn't have to come here tonight. And yet you did. You keep coming back. *(Beat)* Honestly, I don't think that's what you're scared of, not caring enough.

WILLIAM: Then what am I scared of?

BETSY: I think you may be scared of caring too much.

WILLIAM: Where's the middle ground? Where I'm not scared of either?

BETSY: If you have a choice in life between not caring enough or caring too much, choose to care too much. You may get hurt from it…but you won't regret it. *(Long silence)* William?

(WILLIAM *says nothing.*)

BETSY: Earth to William?

WILLIAM: Let's do it.

BETSY: What?

WILLIAM: Let's make a baby.

BETSY: Are you sure?

WILLIAM: Yeah. Let's make a baby.

BETSY: Are you serious?

WILLIAM: As serious as a fucking solar flare.

BETSY: Uh…I'm going to assume that's serious.

WILLIAM: It's very serious. People underestimate the effects of geomagnetic storms on the Earth's—

She hugs him.

BETSY: Thank you. THANK YOU.

WILLIAM: Also radio communication is affected by solar flares—

BETSY: William.

WILLIAM: Sorry. *(Beat)* Thank you.

BETSY: For what?

WILLIAM: Just…thank you.

THE FARTHEST EXPLORER: Why are humans so stubborn? They fight so badly for what they want, even if the odds are against them. Like something miraculous will happen if they just believe hard enough. Maybe it's because the Earth is the third planet from the Sun? Yeah. Like, if it were the first or second planet, humans would burst into flames. If it were the fourth planet, humans would freeze. But somehow, Earth is at the perfect distance to sustain life. So maybe that's why humans believe in the miraculous. They practically live on a planet that is so. Huh.

(BETSY and SHOSHANA's loft.)

WILLIAM: Wow you have a great place.

SHOSHANA: Thanks.

WILLIAM: Nice furniture. I feel like I'm sitting in a West Elm catalog.

BETSY: You are. It's all from West Elm. Kinda scary, right?

WILLIAM: Yeah. Scary. A nightmare on West Elm street!

(WILLIAM *and* BETSY *laugh. Not* SHOSHANA.)

SHOSHANA: Well, as my nanna Abrams would say, "are you gonna rub and tug it or what?"

BETSY: Shana!

SHOSHANA: I'm joking, she would never say that…in those words exactly. *(To* WILLIAM*)* But we are working with a narrow window of opportunity here.

WILLIAM: Yeah, sure. Of course. *(Beat)* So, um, I guess I just need a cup? Or, oh, maybe tupperware would be better? You know, to seal in…to keep it fresh…

SHOSHANA: We have a sterile cup for you. Still in the wrapper.

(SHOSHANA *hands* WILLIAM *the cup.)*

WILLIAM: Great.

(SHOSHANA *grandly presents the cup to* WILLIAM.)

SHOSHANA: *(Singing, slowly)*
I went to the doctor,
I went to the mountains—

BETSY: Don't.

(BETSY *takes the cup and hands it to* WILLIAM.)

WILLIAM: Where's your—

(SHOSHANA *points to the bathroom.)*

(WILLIAM *nods and goes into the bathroom, takes one final look at both of them and shuts the door.)*

SHOSHANA: *(Singing)*
I looked to the children,
I drank from the fountain

(SHOSHANA *takes* BETSY's *hand and prods her into a slow dance.)*

SHOSHANA: *(Singing)*
There's more than one answer to these questions
pointing me in crooked line
(Beat) My nanna gave me this song.

BETSY: Yes, I know. It was at your Bat Mitzvah.

SHOSHANA: *(Lost in the memory)* It was at my Bat Mitzvah—

BETSY: I just said that.

SHOSHANA: While all my friends were dancing to the Super-Hora Klezmer Megamix, I was nowhere to be found.

BETSY: I know. And your nanna went looking / for you

SHOSHANA: Yeah she went looking for me and found me in a closet making out with—

BETSY/SHOSHANA: Mira Morgenstern.

SHOSHANA: Good memory. Instead of disowning her favorite granddaughter, nanna Abrams, who was incredibly progressive and also just really hated men in general; bought me the single of *Closer to Fine.* This became my anthem and eventually...

BETSY: Our wedding song.

SHOSHANA: Our wedding song!

(BETSY *and* SHOSHANA *hum along to the memory and continue slow dancing.)*

THE FARTHEST EXPLORER: As I travel through space, I think about my search for aliens. And all the questions I have about it. Questions like who is out here? Who are they and what are they to us? I've spent all my life searching for answers. But as I get closer to the edge of the solar system, I'm starting to realize that's not what's important. If I never find these answers, I think that's okay. Because honestly, it's the questions that keep me going. And because there are no shortage of questions out here, I might just keep going forever. Sweet!

(Some time has passed. BETSY *is lounging on the couch, flipping through magazines.* SHOSHANA *is reading a book.)*

SHOSHANA: Oh damn, Margaret Atwood, damn!

BETSY: Why are you reading *The Handmaid's Tale*?

SHOSHANA: Why do you assume it's *The Handmaid's Tale* just because it's Margaret Atwood. She wrote other books, you know.

BETSY: Okay, I'm sorry. So which book are you reading?

SHOSHANA: *(Obviously) The Handmaid's Tale.*

BETSY: Shana!

SHOSHANA: It's so good!

BETSY: Don't you find it just a little weird reading that while we're trying to conceive?

SHOSHANA: No weirder than your childhood friend whacking off in our bathroom.

BETSY: Point taken.

SHOSHANA: Do you think he fell asleep or something?

BETSY: He's probably really nervous.

SHOSHANA: Why? It's not like we're in there watching him. He's got privacy and a pile of porn. That's like every guy's dream.

BETSY: You didn't have to buy him a sampler pack.

SHOSHANA: I don't know what he likes. He could be really freaky.

BETSY: William is not freaky. He's very…straight laced.

SHOSHANA: Those are the ones who are really freaky.

BETSY: What's in the sampler pack?

SHOSHANA: Barely legal, Milfs, Big and Tall, Short and Small…

BETSY: What if he's not into that? And now he thinks WE think he's into that?

SHOSHANA: Bets…guys CAN and WILL masturbate to anything.

BETSY: No. You think?

SHOSHANA: Yes! If all we had was a copy of Little Women in there, he would find a way to masturbate to it.

BETSY: We DO have a copy of Little Women in there.

SHOSHANA: Oh shit. You're right. God, what if he's stroking himself as Beth is dying from scarlet fever?

BETSY: That's terrible.

SHOSHANA: I know. Poor Beth.

Betsy knocks on the bathroom door.

BETSY: William? Just checking in on you. Do you need anything?

WILLIAM: No, I'm good. I'm actually reading your copy of *Little Women*. Hope you don't mind.

SHOSHANA: *(Yelling)* YOU CAN KEEP IT!

(WILLIAM *comes out of the bathroom.*)

WILLIAM: She dies. Beth dies in the book.

(FREDDY *appears.*)

FREDDY: William.

WILLIAM: Life is like that, you know?

FREDDY: William!

WILLIAM: ...So fleeting...

FREDDY: William!

WILLIAM: What?

FREDDY: Hand me some toilet paper.

(The men's restroom)

(FREDDY's in a stall. WILLIAM has been staring into a mirror.)

FREDDY: Did you hear me?

WILLIAM: Yeah. Toilet paper.

(WILLIAM goes into the next stall and rolls the toilet paper over to FREDDY.)

FREDDY: Jesus! I said "hand it to me", not "roll it on the dirty fucking floor!" What's wrong with you?

WILLIAM: You know what I was thinking—

FREDDY: *(Singing the melody to Beethoven's 5th Symphony)* NOBODY CARES!

WILLIAM: I was thinking about Betsy and Shoshana, when I was in their bathroom.

FREDDY: Oh! Masturbating?

WILLIAM: Donating my sperm.

FREDDY: Why are you still thinking about that? That was nine weeks ago!

WILLIAM: I know.

FREDDY: You guys are nearing the end of your first trimester. I've been tracking.

WILLIAM: Well that isn't weird or anything.

FREDDY: You know what else isn't weird? I had a dream about them the other night. They wanted me to "donate" my sperm as well.

WILLIAM: Dammit Freddy! Please don't have sex dreams about Bets and Shoshana.

FREDDY: I mean, I can say I won't but then I'd be lying.

WILLIAM: Freddy—

FREDDY: C'mon, you know we'll masturbate to anything.

WILLIAM: I know!

FREDDY: What did you masturbate to?

(Silence)

WILLIAM: *Little Women.*

(Long silence)

FREDDY: Beth dies you know.

WILLIAM: I know.

FREDDY: Scarlet fever. Poor Beth. She couldn't even lift her sewing needle at the end. *(A sniffle)* Oh fuck.

WILLIAM: Are you crying?

(A toilet flush. FREDDY *exits his stall.)*

FREDDY: Beth is dead!

WILLIAM: Why are you so upset?

FREDDY: Because she died a virgin. Not once did she know the pleasure of purposeful touching. And THAT is the tragedy of *Little Women.*

(Beat)

WILLIAM: That is NOT the tragedy of Little Women.

FREDDY: If you say so.

WILLIAM: I almost left without doing it. That book made me so sad. But I mustered up the courage and I went back in.

FREDDY: Atta boy.

WILLIAM: And…this may sound really strange, but I was weeping. I was…masturbating and weeping.

(Beat)

FREDDY: Still waiting for the strange part.

WILLIAM: Freddy!

FREDDY: Listen, I would love to discuss masturbation with you all day long in the men's restroom, especially at the place of our employment, but I sense you have a point that you're sluggishly trying to make?

WILLIAM: I just…when I was in their bathroom reading Little Women, it made me think about family. And for the past nine weeks I've been constantly thinking about this, about the March family gathering around a table enjoying each other's company, even though they're super poor. And I'm thinking maybe I want that?

FREDDY: You want to be super poor?

WILLIAM: No. Don't you get it? They made the most out of what little they had. Listen. Growing up, both my parents worked at night. There was no gathering around a dinner table, no one asking how my day went. I'm not complaining. They worked hard to put food on the table.

FREDDY: *(Solemn)* A table for one.

WILLIAM: *(Annoyed)* Yes, Freddy. A table for one. Thanks for pointing that out. The fact is I'm scared that if I sit down to a family dinner, I might like it. Like a lot. And that might lead to another dinner and another. And all of sudden I realize I've given up on my dreams.

FREDDY: You know how you're tracking Voyager 1 right now?

WILLIAM: Yeah.

FREDDY: You've forgotten there are two Voyagers.

WILLIAM: I haven't forgotten. Of course there are two Voyagers.

FREDDY: Is Voyager 2 less important because it won't be the first to reach interstellar space?

WILLIAM: No.

FREDDY: Right. Some of us aren't meant to be Voyager 1. *(Pointing at* WILLIAM*)* Some of us have to be Voyager 2. But Voyager 2 did amazing stuff that Voyager 1 never did. Like sending back rare photos of the outer planets. Plus it will eventually leave the solar system like its sibling. William, Voyager 2 is proof that you can have both. It just means doing it a little slower.

WILLIAM: They're already selecting key personnel for Mars. I'm already behind.

FREDDY: I'm not saying you should fire your de-orbiting thrusters. I'm saying spend a few hours with the girls. Check up on the baby. You might like it.

WILLIAM: You think so?

FREDDY: Yeah, I do. Look, they said you could be Uncle William. No strings attached. Take advantage of it.

WILLIAM: What about Voyager?

FREDDY: Voyager's fine. You said yourself there's nothing to do but monitor its heartbeat.

WILLIAM: Maybe you're right. Maybe I should see them.

FREDDY: Freddy is always right. Go see them. The sooner the better.

WILLIAM: Well, they do have a check up today.

FREDDY: Perfect. Meet them there. Go.

WILLIAM: Are you sure?

FREDDY: Dude, I've got everything under control.

(Woosh. THE FARTHEST EXPLORER *appears.)*

THE FARTHEST EXPLORER: Okay I'm entering the bow shock! It's the only thing left between me and interstellar space! Wow, to think I was built with enough equipment to only observe Saturn and Jupiter. I was never meant to go any farther. But my designers ignored those instructions. I'm here because they never gave up hope! Someone told them no and they just kept thinking YES! And they put that yes into me. I am YES! I am ALL YES!!!!

(A doctor's office)

*(*BETSY *and* SHOSHANA *sit.* SHOSHANA *is doing a crossword puzzle.)*

SHOSHANA: What's a five letter word for the phrase "I have no idea!"

BETSY: Got me.

SHOSHANA: Can you at least try?

BETSY: No, that's the answer. Got me.

*(*SHOSHANA *counts.)*

SHOSHANA: Okay, that right there, what you just did? Really fucking sexy.

*(*WILLIAM *enters.)*

BETSY: William.

WILLIAM: Hi. Sorry, I know you weren't expecting me.

SHOSHANA: Is something wrong?

WILLIAM: No, not at all. You shared your prenatal calendar with me and I saw you had an appointment today. I thought I'd pop on by…

BETSY: That's great. This is just a boring ol' checkup though.

SHOSHANA: Yeah you should've waited two weeks. That's when we get our first ultrasound.

WILLIAM: Oh okay, I'll come back in two weeks. *(He heads for the exit.)*

BETSY: William! Get back here. Stay.

WILLIAM: Okay.

BETSY: It's nice having all of us together. Right?

SHOSHANA: It is. We're glad you're here. *(She goes back to her crossword.)*

WILLIAM: Thanks. Yep, I'm here. And you're here.

SHOSHANA: We're all here.

(WILLIAM nervously meanders.)

WILLIAM: *(Re: SHOSHANA's crossword)* Alpaca.

SHOSHANA: What?

WILLIAM: Twenty-seven across. Alpaca.

SHOSHANA: THANKS WILLIAM.

WILLIAM: You bet.

(WILLIAM's phone rings.)

WILLIAM: Oh, that's my office. Sorry I have to answer this. *(Stepping out)* Yeah?

FREDDY: *(Freaking out)* WILLIAM!!!!!

WILLIAM: Jesus Freddy! What is wrong?

FREDDY: OH MY GOD WE LOST HER!

WILLIAM: What? Who?

FREDDY: We lost Voyager, dummy!

WILLIAM: What? That's impossible. Are you sure?

FREDDY: Yes! JPL called. Said they lost track of her. Same on our end. Haven't told them anything yet. You have to come back now.

WILLIAM: Okay, I'm leaving.

FREDDY: NOW!!!

WILLIAM: I heard you!

FREDDY: NOW!!!!

WILLIAM: SHUT UP! *(He hangs up.)* Emergency at work. Gotta go. Sorry, I'll call you later. Bye. *(He exits.)*

BETSY: You think William's acting a little—

SHOSHANA: *(Without looking up)* YES.

BETSY: Do you even know what I was going to ask—

SHOSHANA: Strange. You want to know if he's acting strange.

BETSY: Yeah, he is acting strange. I wonder what the emergency is.

SHOSHANA: Perhaps it has something to do with an alpaca.

(The shaking grows.)

THE FARTHEST EXPLORER: *(Trying to keep it together)* WHY IS THERE SO MUCH SHAKING? IS THERE SUPPOSED TO BE THIS MUCH SHAKING? Okay, be calm. Be calm. *(She closes her eyes.)* Seashores…tree with daffodils…the Grand Tetons…an old man with beard and glasses…a group of children around a globe…a nursing mother… *(Beat)* What if I don't make it? No one's ever made it this far. Will I survive the bow shock? I have to I just have to I mean I spent thirty five freakin years out here I can't just vaporize right now in my moment of glory! *(Opening her eyes)* WHY DIDN'T ANYONE TELL ME THERE'D BE SO MUCH SHAKING?!!!! *(Trying to concentrate)*

SAND DUNES! CALIBRATION CIRCLE! SOLAR LOCATION MAP! SAND DUNES! Did I say that already? Whatever. AN ELEPHANT! A CAT'S MEOW! BEETHOVEN! A BABY'S CRY! A HEARTBEAT! LAUGHTER! HEARTBEAT! LAUGHTER! HEARTB—

(THE FARTHEST EXPLORER *disappears. Darkness. Silence)*

(WILLIAM'*s office)*

WILLIAM: Telemetry is dead. Shit!

FREDDY: JPL is freaking out on us!

WILLIAM: No signal on channel 18. Shit!

FREDDY: Just calm down and think. What can we do?

WILLIAM: Goldstone, Madrid and Canberra networks show nothing. Shit!

FREDDY: Stop saying shit! Think!

(WILLIAM *checks his computer.)*

WILLIAM: Nothing. There's nothing…

FREDDY: Come on. There's got to be something.

WILLIAM: I'm honestly at a loss. Freddy, I don't know what we're gonna do.

(Beat)

FREDDY: Shit!

(Week 10)

(Split scene: WILLIAM *works the white board as* FREDDY *snacks.* BETSY *and* SHOSHANA *are in their loft.* SHOSHANA *rubs* BETSY'*s feet.)*

BETSY: Oh God please rub my feet forever.

SHOSHANA: Do not get used to this.

BETSY: Too late. You're the best foot rubber ever. You're the foot rubberer.

SHOSHANA: Ha ha.

BETSY: The big rubowski.

SHOSHANA: Yep, I seem to remember this is what you're like at ten weeks. If we make it past this, I shudder to think what I'm in store for.

BETSY: Aye, there's the rub.

SHOSHANA: Okay please stop.

(Shift)

FREDDY: That won't work.

WILLIAM: Can I at least finish it first?

FREDDY: I already did it in my head. Not gonna work.

WILLIAM: Just let me do it!

FREDDY: I'll make a bet with you. If I'm right, you have to give me a piggy back ride to the vending machine.

WILLIAM: I will never in my hopefully long adult life, make that bet with you.

FREDDY: Afraid you'll lose?

WILLIAM: No, just afraid of you humping my back for twelve and a half yards to the vending machine. *(He finishes the algorithm.)* Dammit, it's wrong. *(He erases everything.)*

FREDDY: Good thing you didn't make that bet.

(Week 11)

SHOSHANA: Come on, I don't want to be late for this ultrasound.

BETSY: Well they can't start without me.

SHOSHANA: Come on, we've been waiting eleven weeks for this.

BETSY: We've been waiting years for this.

SHOSHANA: Yes, years. So come on! We might even get to hear the baby's heartbeat.

(Shift)

(WILLIAM *is reading a printout.)*

WILLIAM: We are so screwed. Once I tell JPL, that's it.

FREDDY: Let's just ignore them.

WILLIAM: Have you lost your mind?

FREDDY: Listen to me. We tell them our heartbeat is getting a slight signal from Voyager and the data is still downloading. That buys us some time.

WILLIAM: But that's…that's lying.

FREDDY: Yes, exactly! I knew you'd get it.

(A text alert. WILLIAM *checks his phone.)*

FREDDY: Who is it? Is it JPL? Throw the phone out the window.

WILLIAM: JPL doesn't text people, dummy. It's Bets. *(On the phone)* Hey Bets. I got your text. What's up?

FREDDY: Oh great, sure. Call your friend. Don't mind me. I'll just be over in the corner looking for a new career.

WILLIAM: What? Really? Okay, sure. I'm listening. *(Beat)* Is that…is that…

FREDDY: What? Why are you making that face?

WILLIAM: Listen.

(WILLIAM *puts the call on the speakerphone.)*

(We hear an infant's heartbeat.)

FREDDY: Is that…

WILLIAM: It's…it's…

FREDDY: Baby…

WILLIAM: Holy shit. I don't know what to say. Bets—

BETSY: *(Through the speakerphone)* Oh, hey the doctor's calling me on the other line. I'll call you back. Bye.

WILLIAM: Bye. Did you hear that? It was a heartbeat.

FREDDY: Yeah. Wow. *(Beat)* I mean, it's not the heartbeat we're looking for right now, but…ah fuck it. Congratulations man.

WILLIAM: Thanks. I helped make that. *(Points to himself)* This guy.

(Week 12)

(SHOSHANA speaks into a voice recorder as BETSY watches. WILLIAM enters.)

SHOSHANA: *(Into the recorder)* So, my little one…hear my voice and know that you can be whatever you want to be. Don't let anyone say you can't…even though you'll be born into a world where everyone will do just that. As Margaret Atwood once said—

BETSY: Really, babe?

SHOSHANA: I'm just preparing our child.

BETSY: *(Noticing WILLIAM)* Oh William.

WILLIAM: Sorry, you had your back door open.

BETSY: We prop it open to cool down the kitchen. August in the city, you know?

WILLIAM: Yeah, August. That's when Voyager was supposed to…sorry I haven't been around the past few weeks. Been busy at work.

BETSY: I'm sorry about Voyager.

SHOSHANA: Yeah, did you ever find out what happened?

WILLIAM: All we know is it should've crossed over into interstellar space by now. But we can't confirm until we get a heartbeat. I should've known better.

BETSY: You had no idea this was going to happen.

WILLIAM: We knew there'd be risks. I should've...I
don't know. *(Beat)* So I see you're recording messages.

BETSY: A memento for the baby.

WILLIAM: That's one lucky baby.

BETSY: *(To* WILLIAM*)* You should record something.

WILLIAM: Me? Oh, I don't know.

BETSY: *(To* SHOSHANA*)* Don't you think he should?

WILLIAM: I don't want to confuse the baby.

SHOSHANA: Too late. Freddy's already recorded
something.

WILLIAM: Freddy? When was he here?

SHOSHANA: He dropped off a fully assembled crib
yesterday. He said he couldn't wait. I strangely didn't
have the heart to crush his little man-spirits.

BETSY: So, William? How about it? It'll cheer you up, I
know it will.

SHOSHANA: Go ahead.

(SHOSHANA *hands the recorder to* WILLIAM.*)*

WILLIAM: I don't really know what to say.

BETSY: You can do it.

WILLIAM: I... *(To them)* Wow, I'm kinda nervous.

BETSY: Start with your name.

WILLIAM: *(Clearing his throat)* I...this is William. I know
your...parents. And I...umm...I like space. Like a lot.
And...I used to keep clippings of the Voyager space
program in a scrapbook. Um...clippings are cut from
paper, which is what we used to write on.

SHOSHANA: I think paper will still be around.

WILLIAM: Right. *(Into the recorder)* So Voyager. What
can I tell you about Voyager? Um...well, it carries

different greetings. In case it makes contact with other forms of intelligent life. *(Beat)* I never thought much about greetings until I worked on Voyager. But greetings are important. It signifies the start of a human connection. In this day and age, people come in and out of each other's lives all the time. But the ones who stick around…one day you'll realize just how important they are. How much they matter to you. *(Beat)* I'm looking forward to meeting you. To making a proper greeting. Until then… *(He turns off the recorder.)* Was that okay?

BETSY: It was perfect.

WILLIAM: I think I rambled a bit. I haven't slept.

BETSY: It's okay.

WILLIAM: So tomorrow's a big day, right?

BETSY: Yeah. We'll find out if the coast is clear.

SHOSHANA: All systems go. That's what they say, right?

WILLIAM: That's what they say, yep. *(Beat)* Well, I just stopped by to see if you needed anything.

BETSY: I think we're good. *(Reading him)* Do you need anything?

WILLIAM: No, I'm good. We're all good. Yep. I just… needed to get out of the office for a while. Okay. Well, I should go.

SHOSHANA: Hey William. We were about to sit down for dinner.

BETSY: Yeah, join us. You look like you haven't eaten in a while.

WILLIAM: Oh…I…thanks. But I don't want to impose.

SHOSHANA: It's just dinner.

WILLIAM: A sit down dinner. Like the March family.

SHOSHANA: Who?

BETSY: *(To* SHOSHANA*)* From *Little Women.*

SHOSHANA: Oh, right. That book we used to own.

BETSY: *(To* WILLIAM*)* So what do you say William?

(Beat)

WILLIAM: I…no. I want to. But I really can't. Raincheck?

BETSY: Sure. Raincheck.

FREDDY: So what do you want me to tell JPL?

*(*WILLIAM*'s office)*

*(*WILLIAM *and* FREDDY *are drinking beers.)*

WILLIAM: Huh?

FREDDY: JPL. You're right, we should give them an update.

WILLIAM: Can we talk about something else? Just for five minutes? Something other than space?

FREDDY: Sure. So, how are things with "the ladies?"

WILLIAM: By "ladies" you mean Bets and Shoshana?

FREDDY: Well those are the ONLY ladies in your life, so, YEAH.

WILLIAM: Well you should know. You dropped off a crib for them, didn't you?

FREDDY: I did. You don't have to say it. I know it was thoughtful of me.

WILLIAM: Listen, I applaud your generosity and enthusiasm for this baby, but you don't give them a crib at twelve weeks.

FREDDY: Why, because of the miscarriages?

WILLIAM: Wow. Your complete absence of tact amazes me.

FREDDY: Listen, I know it's a difficult subject for everyone, but I wanted to do something hopeful. I'm sorry.

WILLIAM: Just try to be a little more sensitive next time. Please?

FREDDY: I hear ya cluckin, big chicken.

(Lights up on BETSY *and* SHOSHANA *at their loft.* SHOSHANA *is doing yoga.)*

SHOSHANA: You wanna do some warrior ones or twos with me?

BETSY: I'm fine.

SHOSHANA: Are you sure?

BETSY: YES. The doctor's gonna call with news either way.

SHOSHANA: Okay. *(Deep breath)* Okay.

BETSY: I don't think yoga will change anything.

SHOSHANA: Right. I know. *(Beat)* I think I'm gonna do some warrior ones if you don't mind.

(Shift to WILLIAM *and* FREDDY.*)*

FREDDY: I think we should get really drunk and then you can give me a piggy back ride to the vending machine for some snackage.

WILLIAM: What is it with you and piggy back rides? What are you, five?

FREDDY: I can't help it if constant failure reminds me of my childhood.

WILLIAM: Just stop with the piggy back rides.

FREDDY: C'mon, I'm craving some Chee-Tos.

WILLIAM: No piggyback rides. *(Beat)* Also, why are you saying Cheetos like that?

FREDDY: Like what?

WILLIAM: With a hard "t." You're saying Chee-Tos.

FREDDY: That's how you're supposed to say it.

WILLIAM: No, you say it like this: "cheetos". With a slight "d" sound.

(Shift to BETSY *and* SHOSHANA, *currently in a warrior one yoga pose.)*

SHOSHANA: You know the more I do yoga the more I realize I'm really not meant to do yoga.

BETSY: Then stop doing yoga.

SHOSHANA: If I stop, it wins.

(Beat)

BETSY: Hey. So I was thinking maybe...maybe we should talk about names. For the baby.

SHOSHANA: Are you sure?

BETSY: Yeah. Yeah, I'm sure. Let's do it.

SHOSHANA: Alright. This is great. *(Beat)* Oh, Charlotte, you know, my sous chef? When she was naming her baby, she made categories like "timeless names" and "old lady names" and um...oh, "names to live up to".

BETSY: What's a name to live up to?

SHOSHANA: Joy. I've met several Joys who do not live up to their name.

BETSY: Maybe we should revisit our old list of names? For inspiration.

SHOSHANA: I'm game.

BETSY: Remember any?

SHOSHANA: Um, there was Ella. Hazel. Rose! Not Titanic Rose, but like 1920s Broadway actress Rose McClendon.

BETSY: There was a Benjamin. Malcolm.

SHOSHANA: There was Serena.

BETSY: Serena. I feel like there can only be one Serena.

SHOSHANA: Yeah.

BETSY: Oh! Celeste.

SHOSHANA: Celeste. Like a star.

BETSY: Like a star.

SHOSHANA: I bet William would like that. *(Beat)* Do you think he has any names?

BETSY: We could ask but I think he's kinda busy with Voyager.

SHOSHANA: That's true. It's serious over there. William's got algorithms written all over his office. I can't even imagine what's going through his supercomputer brain right now.

WILLIAM: Cheetos.

FREDDY: Chee-Tos.

WILLIAM: Cheetos.

FREDDY: Chee-Tos.

WILLIAM: You're not even trying.

FREDDY: It sounds weird.

WILLIAM: The way you're saying it sounds weird.

FREDDY: Who cares how I say chee-Tos! It's the way I say it!

WILLIAM: Fine, but no one else says it like that.

FREDDY: So no piggy back ride then?

WILLIAM: No!

FREDDY: How about just half way? Drop me off in front of the men's room and I'll go the rest of the way myself.

WILLIAM: I will never be drunk enough to give you even half a piggy back...

FREDDY: ...ride. Say it with me. Piggy Back ride.

WILLIAM: *(Wheels are turning)* Piggy back...piggy back...piggy back...

FREDDY: What are you...why are you...oh my God are you having a stroke right now?

WILLIAM: Piggy Back!

FREDDY: Listen to me very carefully: DO YOU SMELL BURNT TOAST?

WILLIAM: Go get the manual.

FREDDY: What manual?

WILLIAM: What do you mean what manual? THE MANUAL.

FREDDY: Voyager's? But it's so old!

WILLIAM: Just go get it. It's in your office. GO!

(FREDDY runs out the door. WILLIAM logs into his computer. FREDDY re-enters with the manual, throws it down as a plume of dust wafts through the air.)

FREDDY: *(Winded)* Here you go. Holy crap I'm out of shape.

WILLIAM: Your office is next to mine.

FREDDY: There are turns involved, William! Hairpin!

(WILLIAM flips through the manual, finds a page and compares it to what's on his computer.)

FREDDY: *(Still winded)* Before I have this imminent heart attack from running, would you mind telling me what's going on?

WILLIAM: I'm looking up Voyager's com address.

FREDDY: Why? Voyager 1 is gone. Lost in space, Will Robinson.

WILLIAM: I'm not talking about Voyager 1. I'm talking about Voyager 2.

FREDDY: But we didn't lose Voyager 2.

WILLIAM: I know! "Some of us have to be Voyager 2" remember?

FREDDY: Yeah, but I was talking philosophically about life and shit.

WILLIAM: Okay, listen to me very carefully, because I do not have time to repeat this.

FREDDY: Because of your stroke?

WILLIAM: I AM NOT HAVING A STROKE!!! Just listen. There's still a possibility that Voyager 1 is out there, waiting for a signal from us in order to respond with its heartbeat. And it's also possible that the signal we're sending is not strong enough to travel that far a distance from Earth because we've never done that before. Right?

FREDDY: So far everything you're saying is theoretically correct.

WILLIAM: Great. So, what we can do is send our signal to Voyager 2 because it's closer to us. And then we command Voyager 2 to relay our signal to Voyager 1. If Voyager 1 is still out there, it will receive a signal thinking it's from us and respond with a heartbeat, ensuring that we will not go down in history as the guys who lost an entire space probe.

FREDDY: Dude, you're gonna piggy back the signal using Voyager 2 YOU ARE FUCKING BRILLIANT! Actually I'M BRILLIANT because the piggy back ride was my idea.

WILLIAM: (Typing) Okay, so I've locked onto Voyager 2's com address. And I'm changing the relay address to point to Voyager 1's. Okay. Alright. Hopefully this will work. This has gotta work. Okay, ready?

FREDDY: Ready.

(WILLIAM *taps his keyboard.)*

WILLIAM: Okay. It's sent. Now we wait thirty six hours for an answer.

FREDDY: Wow, space is really anticlimactic. I guess I have time to get some more Chee-Tos.

(*Flashes of light.* BETSY *and* SHOSHANA *lumber over to their loft.* BETSY *lies on the couch.* SHOSHANA *puts a blanket on her, takes the baby book and exits.)*

(BETSY *and* SHOSHANA's *loft)*

(*A doorbell.* BETSY *slowly gets up from the couch and opens the door.)*

(WILLIAM *enters carrying a laptop.)*

WILLIAM: Hi.

BETSY: Hi.

WILLIAM: I'm…

BETSY: I know. Want some coffee?

WILLIAM: It's like nine o'clock at night.

BETSY: I didn't realize I slept so long.

WILLIAM: It's good that you're sleeping.

BETSY: Yeah, getting plenty of rest. It's easy after a long cry. *(Beat)* I kinda wish I was in space right now. I saw this video on the internet, this astronaut was demonstrating how tears don't fall in space. That sounds nice, doesn't it? Not being able to cry?

WILLIAM: You can still cry in space. You just have to absorb them with a towel otherwise they'd just float around forever. Or if there's a sudden loss of cabin pressure, your tears would boil.

BETSY: Thanks for cheering me up.

(BETSY *and* WILLIAM *laugh.*)

WILLIAM: Listen, I wanted to show you something if you think you're up for it.

BETSY: Okay.

(WILLIAM *opens his laptop.*)

WILLIAM: Don't let this intimidate you.

BETSY: What am I looking at?

WILLIAM: You. Well, a data representation of you. And this is me.
I've been analyzing this data and I think I've found a way to get some better results.

BETSY: William—

WILLIAM: And look here. I produced data models from this inference engine I wrote and…the models hold up quite well. We just have to track everything, and I mean EVERYTHING. That's key—

BETSY: William, it's over.

WILLIAM: No, it's totally doable. First, if we change up both our diets to make sure we—

BETSY: William.

WILLIAM: If you just look at these models, it's very simple…

BETSY: It's not simple, William. It will never be simple. Not with me.

WILLIAM: I don't mean simple. I mean doable. It's doable. The math proves it.

BETSY: William, stop. Maybe your life runs on science and numbers but it doesn't do me any good. The numbers don't work for me. Do you understand?

WILLIAM: I don't understand why we can't try again? I'm showing you a solution—

BETSY: You know how many times I've tried and failed?

(Beat)

WILLIAM: I don't understand. The night before your check up, you seemed healthy.

BETSY: It's called a "missed miscarriage." It happens without anyone knowing it.

WILLIAM: I'm sorry.

BETSY: You always say sorry. Stop saying sorry.

WILLIAM: Betsy, we were so close. I don't want to give up.

BETSY: I am not giving up. I'm giving in. To the inevitable. *(Beat)* I warned you this might not work.

WILLIAM: I know but I can't help but think—

BETSY: Stop William.

WILLIAM: I know we can do this. We can produce another outcome. This time will be different.

BETSY: Different? I'm not a data model that you can tweak for a better result. This is my body.

WILLIAM: I know that.

BETSY: No you don't know that. You don't know what it's like having a miscarriage.

WILLIAM: You're right I don't know how it feels. I can't possibly know. I really wish I did.

BETSY: Oh you do? You wish you knew how it felt to lose a baby?

WILLIAM: I didn't mean it like that.

BETSY: You want to feel the isolation from your friends? The ones who have kids? The ones that stop offering to show photos of their newborn because they feel bad for you? *(Beat)* Or maybe you want to know the different ways to get a miscarriage out of your system? Because, you know, when you have one, it doesn't magically disappear. But don't worry, there are options available. You can take a pill to kickstart the process. Or go for the deluxe package which comes with a metal scraper, a suction tube and some very happy drugs. I suggest the deluxe package, because those drugs...oh man, those drugs are the best. They turn you into a regular comedian, cracking jokes in the operating chair. Laughing the hardest you've ever laughed in a long time. And for a moment you forget. Until the nurse who's holding your hand tells you to cry now instead of holding back those tears for later. *(Beat)* Or maybe you want to know what it's like after that? When weeks later the results from that test the doctor ordered, the one to see if you can actually carry a baby to term, when those results are posted online. And right there on the screen is the sex of your unborn baby. YOUR UNBORN... *(Beat)* And then you know specifically what you lost. And you get to relive that pain all over again. And that's when you realize you'll always be haunted by your miscarriages. *(Beat)* How's that William? Was that descriptive enough for you?

WILLIAM: Tell me what to do.

BETSY: Go home.

WILLIAM: Sure. I'll come by tomorrow to check up on you.

BETSY: No.

WILLIAM: Okay. Well, how about in a few days?

BETSY: I don't think I can see you right now.

WILLIAM: Bets.

BETSY: William, I know you feel this attachment. It's natural. But don't forget, you decided not to be involved for a reason.

WILLIAM: I'm sorry I put my career ahead of this.

BETSY: Don't be sorry. That's your dream. Why would you want to get involved now? Spare yourself the hurt.

WILLIAM: No. Don't do this. Don't push me away. I'm here for you now.

BETSY: You can't just pick and choose when you want to be there for me. I accept the fact that we changed. I knew that when I reached out to you.

WILLIAM: But it was so effortless, how we picked up right where we left off. After all those years. Don't deny our friendship!

BETSY: I'm not denying it! But you're acting as though I needed it! I didn't need your friendship William. I just needed your sperm!

(WILLIAM *says nothing.*)

BETSY: William. I'm sorry.

(WILLIAM *gathers his things.*)

BETSY: William—

WILLIAM: No, you're right. I should've never pushed this. I'll leave you alone.

BETSY: William.

(FREDDY *appears.*)

FREDDY: Will we hear from Voyager 1 tonight?

(WILLIAM's *office*)

(FREDDY *shakes the magic eight ball.*)

FREDDY: (*Reading*) "Reply hazy try again." FUCK YOU MAGIC EIGHT BALL!

WILLIAM: Freddy.

FREDDY: Sorry. Voyager's late.

WILLIAM: I know.

FREDDY: We should've heard from it by now.

WILLIAM: I know.

FREDDY: Like an hour ago.

WILLIAM: I know.

FREDDY: Voyager 1 is gone and it's never coming back. Just like my ex wife.

WILLIAM: Jesus, don't do this right now. I can't handle it.

FREDDY: Oh YOU can't handle it? I've had to put up with you for months about all this baby stuff and now your fight with Betsy and blah blah blah go fuck yourself.

WILLIAM: Okay, okay. You're right. You've been putting up with all my shit. It's not fair. I'm sorry.

FREDDY: Freddy accepts your apology. *(Beat)* Listen to me. You're afraid.

WILLIAM: Afraid? I'm not afraid. Why would you say that?

FREDDY: Here at work, you're brilliant. When the wheels start turning in that noggin of yours, you're fearless. But everything else, your personal life, you're terrified of it.

WILLIAM: That's absolutely ridiculous. I'm not terrified.

FREDDY: You totally are. That's why you had that nightmare right before Betsy came back into your life. It wasn't about work, it was about Betsy. It's like you have a built-in early warning system.

WILLIAM: Yeah well I should've listened to my gut. It knew. We lost Voyager. We lost the baby. The moment

I thought I could actually have it both ways…and then this happens.

FREDDY: That's why you don't go all in. You play it safe with your personal life. You played it safe with Betsy.

WILLIAM: Are you joking right now? I went all in with Betsy. JESUS CHRIST I MASTURBATED TO *LITTLE WOMEN!*

FREDDY: Yeah and you changed your mind about wanting to be involved but you didn't have the guts to ask them. And when Betsy lost the baby, you probably felt somewhat relieved.

WILLIAM: That's not true!

(FREDDY shakes the magic eight ball.)

FREDDY: *(Reading)* "It is decidedly so"

WILLIAM: FUCK YOU MAGIC EIGHT BALL! And fuck you Freddy! You're an asshole, you know that?

FREDDY: Good, get it all out, man.

WILLIAM: And who are you to judge on involvement?

FREDDY: Hey I was just trying to be honest with you.

WILLIAM: No one asked for your honesty. And no one asked you to get involved with this.

FREDDY: I was just trying to help.

WILLIAM: Help? Like dropping off a crib? Recording messages for the baby? I mean it's like you wanted this more than I did!

FREDDY: Well maybe I did!

WILLIAM: What the hell is that supposed to mean?

(FREDDY says nothing.)

WILLIAM: No don't get quiet now. Why the interest in this?

(FREDDY feeds his face with Cheetos.)

WILLIAM: Stop eating those Cheetos and TELL ME.

FREDDY: Carmen and I…we talked about getting pregnant for years, but she kept putting it off. I thought she didn't want to have children. I kept pressing her about it until she finally told me she did want to have children. She just didn't want to have them with me. That's why we got divorced. *(Beat)* You're lucky William. To have someone who wants your child. You're lucky. *(He grabs some magazines and heads for the door.)*

WILLIAM: Where are you going?

FREDDY: It's pooptime for ol' Freddy.

(Shift to BETSY and SHOSHANA's apartment.)

(BETSY is on the couch with her laptop.)

SHOSHANA: Babe, come to bed. It's really late.

BETSY: Or really early.

SHOSHANA: What are you doing?

BETSY: Catching up on work.

SHOSHANA: You're supposed to be on break.

BETSY: Everything's piling up. I have agendas to approve, constituency lists to maintain, lot's to do.

SHOSHANA: There will always be agendas to approve and lists to maintain. Take a break.

BETSY: I just said there's lots to do.

SHOSHANA: Take a break.

BETSY: Five minutes.

SHOSHANA: Fifteen.

BETSY: Five.

SHOSHANA: Ten.

BETSY: Five.

SHOSHANA: Five and that's my final offer.

(SHOSHANA *shuts* BETSY's *laptop.*)

BETSY: I don't mind doing work.

SHOSHANA: You don't need to do work right now.

BETSY: Yes I do.

SHOSHANA: Why? To distract yourself? I can do that.
I'm a great distraction.

BETSY: No. I need to do my work. I know how to do my
work. I'm good at it.

SHOSHANA: I know you are.

BETSY: I know how to mail merge and freeze columns
and I can even do pivot tables! And not many people
can do pivot tables, but I can. I can do them. I can do
pivot tables. Please just let me do my pivot tables!

SHOSHANA: Fine, you can do your pivot tables. I don't
even know what those are. But take a break first.

BETSY: I'm sorry I'm a mess.

SHOSHANA: It's okay. You're my mess. *(Beat)* Tell me
what I can do for you.

BETSY: You're Shoshana Abrams. You always know
what to do.

(Beat)

SHOSHANA: Maybe it's time…you know, to revisit…

BETSY: Go ahead, you can say it.

SHOSHANA: Adoption is a viable alternative.

BETSY: Are you ready to trade in one kind of setback
for another?

SHOSHANA: I mean, besides the long waiting period,
enormous costs, and countries that won't allow us to
adopt…what could go wrong?

BETSY: Everything could go wrong.

SHOSHANA: I was joking.

BETSY: Everything has gone wrong!

SHOSHANA: Not everything.

BETSY: Look at me. I'm living proof.

SHOSHANA: Should I leave you alone?

BETSY: Why are you with me? I honestly think you'd be better off with someone else.

SHOSHANA: I can't believe you just said that.

(Off BETSY'*s silence:)*

SHOSHANA: Listen to me. I don't want to compare pain…but I feel it too. Especially with this one. I hurt as well. I hurt differently than you, but I still hurt. And for the most part, I hurt silently because I don't want to upset you. And I did not do all that…for you to stand here right now and wonder if I'd be better off. Because I've never wondered that. I still believe in us.

BETSY: You do? You really believe in us, after all this?

SHOSHANA: Bets…what's a… *(Counting in her head)* … seventeen letter word for yes?

(Off BETSY'*s silence)*

SHOSHANA: Abso-fucking-lutely.

(Shift to WILLIAM'*s office. He is speaking into a recorder.)*

WILLIAM: …And Voyager's golden record also contains a cat's meow. The music of Beethoven. A baby's cry. *(He turns the recorder off. He turns the recorder on.)* I should've stopped these recordings for you when Betsy…when we lost you. I don't know why I'm still talking to you… *(He checks to see if the coast is clear.)* Freddy's right. I'm scared. I wake up in the middle of the night, sweating with anxiety. Scared there's not enough time to do the things I want to do. Something significant. And there's no room for anything else. But then Betsy and Shoshana happened. And you happened. *(Beat)* And for a fleeting moment, you made me less terrified of my life. I wish I could've met you. I wish I could've said—

(A faint beeping)

(WILLIAM cautiously checks his computer.)

(Another beep)

(Beep)

(Beep)

(BEEP)

WILLIAM: HOLY SHIT!!!! *(Into the recorder)* Oh sorry, you didn't hear that.

(FREDDY enters,)

FREDDY: Oh man, pooptime is my favorite time in the whole wide—

WILLIAM: It's back! Voyager is back!

FREDDY: SHUDDUP.

WILLIAM: Listen!

(BEEP)

FREDDY: Did you check the telemetry?

WILLIAM: Yep, RTGs are responding.

FREDDY: And the Deep Space Network?

WILLIAM: Channel 18 at 8.4 GHz!

FREDDY: 8.4GHz! YES THAT'S VOYAGER!!!!

WILLIAM: YES!!! We have a heartbeat! We have a heartbeat!!!!

FREDDY & WILLIAM: WE HAVE A HEARTBEAT!!!!

(WILLIAM stops. He cries.)

FREDDY: Umm…are you okay?

(WILLIAM *cries harder.*)

FREDDY: Umm, Freddy does not know how to deal with this.

(WILLIAM's *crying is deep. Something that has been stirring inside him for a very long time.*)

FREDDY: Do you…do you want some Chee-Tos?

WILLIAM: *(Through his tears)* I just…we've been waiting for this for so long…and I was so worried we lost it. I just wanted Voyager to be safe. And it is and it's finally out there. It's out there in the great unknown. And I feel so…proud. I'm so PROUD. *(He grabs his bag.)*

FREDDY: Where are you going? We have to call JPL.

WILLIAM: You call them. There's something I have to do.

FREDDY: Right now? In our moment of glory?

WILLIAM: Freddy, I cannot waste a second longer.

FREDDY: Well…can I come too?

(THE FARTHEST EXPLORER *appears.*)

THE FARTHEST EXPLORER: HOLY SHIT I MADE IT!!! Sorry for the language. But Holy Shit! I thought I was a goner. So this is it. Wow. Look at that nebula cloud! And that nursery of infant stars over there. The colors. I can't even describe it. No one on Earth has ever seen this. Not the way I'm seeing it right now. *(She takes it all in. A long moment)*

(BETSY *and* SHOSHANA's *loft*)

(SHOSHANA *opens the front door.* BETSY *is nearby.*)

SHOSHANA: William.

WILLIAM: Hi. Is um… *(Seeing* BETSY*)* Hi.

BETSY: Hi.

WILLIAM: I know you said you didn't want to see me. But I wanted to see you. To make sure you're okay. Are you okay?

(Beat)

BETSY: This afternoon I only cried for about an hour. I banged out a couple of pivot tables. And then I had a pint of mint chocolate chip ice cream all to myself. So, progress.

SHOSHANA: Babe...you ate my ice cream?

BETSY: Sorry.

SHOSHANA: That's okay.

BETSY: *(To WILLIAM)* You just keep coming back don't you?

(WILLIAM says nothing.)

BETSY: Good. *(Beat)* What I said to you the last time you were here, I didn't mean it.

WILLIAM: I know.

BETSY: We tried and we got real close. And maybe that was enough for us. But Shoshana and I, we're not done yet.

SHOSHANA: We're exploring options.

BETSY: We'll get what we want. Eventually.

WILLIAM: That sounds like the Betsy I know. *(Beat)* I also came here because something great happened tonight. And I realized I wanted to share the news with...both of you.

(FREDDY enters, out of breath.)

FREDDY: Ho...holy flight of stairs, Batman. *(To WILLIAM)* Dude you ran so fast! Up those stairs!

FREDDY: *(To WILLIAM)* Did you tell them?

WILLIAM: I was about to.

BETSY: Tell us what?

FREDDY: We got a heartbeat from Voyager! It's alive!

WILLIAM: *(To* FREDDY*)* Thanks.

BETSY: That's fantastic!

SHOSHANA: Aww yeah!

*(*FREDDY *and* SHOSHANA *perform a secret handshake.)*

BETSY: *(Re: the handshake)* Wow. *(To* WILLIAM*)* Wait, so does this mean California's next?

WILLIAM: I think so. Yeah. What do you think about that?

BETSY: I think…we should celebrate.

WILLIAM: I would love a celebration. What'd you have in mind?

BETSY: I seem to remember a raincheck. How does dinner sound?

WILLIAM: It's almost midnight.

SHOSHANA: Second dinner.

FREDDY: I'm all about second dinners.

BETSY: William?

WILLIAM: Dinner sounds great.

*(*WILLIAM, BETSY, SHOSHANA, *and* FREDDY *gather around a dinner table.)*

THE FARTHEST EXPLORER: Interstellar means "the space between stars." It'll take about a hundred and forty thousand years to reach the next closest star. *(Beat)* I feel immense joy. But also immense distance. I finally understand how far I've come. *(She looks at* WILLIAM, BETSY, SHOSHANA, *and* FREDDY.*)* Humans came from the stars. Their atoms inherited from a galactic explosion. So it makes sense they'd want to return to the stars. To the home of their ancestors who gave them life. *(She slowly travels around the dinner table.)* And maybe that's why my Golden Record is so important to humans. It actually is their home movie. Yeah. It's meant to show what they were able to make together, in their own space between stars. And I'm here to deliver their home movie…to you. The celestial parents they'll never get to meet. *(Beat)* Can you hear me? On humans' behalf, I'd like to say…we made it. We've found a way back to you. We're your children…and we just wanted to say… *(Beat)* Hello.

(Beep)

(Beep)

(Beep)

[[[END TRANSMISSION]]]